Get Booked!

Attract More Clients & Boost Your Brand Through Business Podcast Guest Appearances

By Dave Mendonca

TABLE OF CONTENTS

FREE RESOURCES TO MAKE YOU A PROFITABLE PODCAST GUEST

Appearing as a guest on an interview-based business podcast can be a game changer.

It can catapult your brand and supply you with an ongoing stream of future clients.

But first, you must have the right preparation to make the above a reality.

After reading **_Get Booked!_**, the free resources will give you an added edge with valuable bonus content to make sure you're ready to profit from your podcast appearances right away.

Don't let your competition master this marketing strategy before you do.

Access the free resources below and start monetizing your podcast interviews today.

www.thestandoutnowpodcast.com/gbfreeresources

Get Booked!

Introduction

The world has changed.

Once upon a time you, the entrepreneur, could place advertisements or appear on television, radio, print and online to promote your brand, product and/or service and hope for a good return.

Back then, the battle for your ideal client's attention wasn't as fierce as it is today.

Now that we're in the social media era, we're bombarded with large amounts of marketing messages every day.

If you're a subject matter expert or CEO looking for exposure or even a public relations agency trying to secure clients with the right media opportunities, it's tough to create any traction because of all the noise out there.

Television isn't as reliable as it used to be because of all the fragmentation with so many channels available and juggernauts like Netflix and other streaming services stealing away eyeballs.

Radio is somewhat staying alive because it's still a staple for older commuters who drive and the medium has also enjoyed a second life with some shows having podcast versions, but mostly when you listen to its terrestrial form, you'll have no control over what you consume.

Print is dying a slow death thanks to the internet which has made it even more dated and irrelevant than ever before.

Then there's online. Sure, there are Facebook ads that can be powerful, but there's a logjam of other social media websites and blogs (hundreds of MILLIONS of them!) that would love your advertising dollars, but can they deliver the results you're looking for?

If you're an entrepreneur, how can you possibly target your ideal audience when it seems like they're being pulled into different directions?

There is an answer.

It's a marketing strategy that massive companies like FedEx, Toyota, Gillette and Home Depot are implementing.

For good reason, it's generating them ongoing sales leads, buyers and brand exposure for days, weeks, months and potentially years to come.

What I'm talking about is podcast marketing.

First off, if you're reading this book, maybe you don't know much about podcasting.

So, what is a podcast?

Basically, it's an on-demand audio file that can be streamed or downloaded from the internet.

It's a new form of radio, but one that you have complete control of when choosing the content you'd like to consume.

Podcasts started to get noticed in 2004 and feature various types of shows from sports to business to comedy to investigative journalism.

So, what's the big deal with podcasts?

Why should you advertise on them?

As you'll discover in this book, podcasts have created incredibly niche and loyal audiences that no other mediums have been able to replicate during these noisy times.

These underground fan bases have grown to such an extent they can't be ignored anymore.

One of the reasons for the rise in popularity is the convenience of podcasts alone have made it a different ballgame where they can now be a part of your everyday life without disrupting your life.

In *Get Booked!* we'll examine a type of podcast marketing that is proving to be profitable for many entrepreneurs.

It's called Podcast Guest Marketing.

It's a strategy used by business heavyweights such as Tony Robbins, Tim Ferriss and Gary Vaynerchuk to name a few.

It's where you or your client (if you're a public relations agency) appear as a guest, mostly for FREE, to promote yourselves or your companies on interview-based business podcasts.

If done right, Podcast Guest Marketing can help you speak directly to your ideal customers and attract ongoing leads and sales for days, weeks, months and years to come.

How do I know?

I've seen it.

Since 2008, off and on, I've been in the podcasting world as a podcast host, an Entrepreneur.com writer, who covered podcasting and interviewed the likes of podcast stars such as James Altucher, Amy Porterfield, Lewis Howes, Farnoosh Torabi, and as the owner of a Toronto-based podcast guest booking agency, Podcast Interview Experts.

Through my experiences, I've watched as my interview subjects and clients leveraged their podcast guest appearances to generate revenue and enhance their brands.

What's exciting is this form of marketing is just in its infant stages.

Podcasts haven't become fully mainstream yet, like TV or radio, which means there's an opportunity.

Yes, there are hundreds of thousands of podcasts out there, but they're not all a fit for you.

As you'll soon find out, if you learn how to find podcasts that are suitable, it could be a game-changer for you and your business.

So, if you're ready to explore a new and affordable way to consistently reach your ideal clients, your adventure begins now.

1

Why You MUST Know Your Ideal Client

It's common sense, right?

Before you start a business, you should have a specific idea of who will buy your stuff.

You'd be surprised how many entrepreneurs fail that test.

It's an important one to ace because when it comes to being placed on interview-based business podcasts, you'll want to know who your audience is, so you can appear on shows that are filled with people who will be interested in your topic and will eventually be your clients.

If you already have a great idea of who your perfect customer is then you can skip this chapter, but if you don't, stick around.

There are so many ways to figure out your client avatar, but first, let's see a bad, better and best example of what one would look like.

Bad

My ideal client is anyone who likes (insert topic).

Better

My ideal client is 35-54 years old, works full-time, has 3 kids, a mortgage and is frustrated and scared every day because she doesn't know where her life is going and needs help to find the information that I'll provide about (insert topic) which will give her clarity.

Best

My ideal client is 36 years old. Her name is Sally and is a lawyer. She's been interested in starting a legal podcast for 6 months but has no clue where to begin. She is a terrific speaker who dabbled with on-air broadcasting in high school when she'd go on the PA system to make morning announcements but decided to put her broadcast dreams to rest because she didn't see a future in it. Now, she's been bitten by the announcing bug again, but she could really use some help to create and launch a podcast because she has no idea what equipment she'll need, how to structure a show and how to promote it to her ideal audience.

As you can see, the avatars became more descriptive as you went along.

The interesting thing about the final example was that you learned about the person's SPECIFIC struggles.

That's the key.

Once you understand the precise pain points of your ideal customer, you'll be able to create products, services and content that will give the solution she's looking for.

In the case of appearing on interviewed-based business podcasts, by knowing the specific challenges of your ideal clients and finding shows that have listeners who share those same challenges, your content will be much more useful to them which can lead them to wanting to find out more about you and ultimately wanting to buy from you.

So, when finding out who your ideal customers are, you really want to dig and ask the following:

What are their dreams and ambitions?

What are their values?

What are their biggest problems and fears?

What don't they like about their current situation?

What books, magazines and websites do they read?

What TV shows do they watch?

What conferences do they attend?

Are they married?

How many kids do they have?

Ideally, you'd like to ask them directly whether it's in person or online.

Basically, the more you know about what makes your ideal clients tick, the better it is for you and them.

By having this knowledge, you'll be in a great position to help them win.

That's all terrific, but where do you find your ideal customers to ask them these questions?

Here are a few options…

- **Social media (LinkedIn, Facebook, Twitter & Instagram)**

- **In person gatherings (Conferences, workshops, school, Meetup.com)**

- **Personal and professional networks (Ask people you know if they can refer you to people that resemble your client avatar)**

Remember, when meeting these people, it's important not to come off as salesy. Always have the mindset that you want to help them

FIRST, so if it's an in person meeting you'd like, offer to buy her a coffee and find out about her organically without any forced sales pitches.

Your job will be to listen carefully to what she's saying, so you can have a great idea of how you can help her down the line.

If you're wondering how you can invite people in the first place, well, if you met someone at a networking event and received her business card, you could email her.

Here's a sample message you could send.

Subject: Hi Lisa, It's Carol. It Was Nice Meeting You...

Hello Lisa,

I hope all is well.

This is Carol Messina of Carol's Rock Star Paint Brushes. We met last night at the Entrepreneurs Unite! networking event.

It was great meeting you.

Thank you for taking the time to chat.

I was really interested in what you had to say about your business, would you have time to have a coffee to discuss further?

I think you're doing some great things and I may have some ideas that could help you even more.

Let me know what you think.

Thanks again and have a great day!

Carol

As long as you can find a way to authentically communicate that you can help that person without selling, you'll have a better chance at securing a meeting.

Emailing is a less intrusive way of getting in touch, so try that.

If you're emailing someone that has been referred to you, don't forget to mention the mutual connection in the subject line. It sounds obvious, but not everyone does it.

Meeting your potential clients is a terrific way to find out what they truly need.

By having an in-depth understanding of your ideal customer, you'll find once you're ready to appear on specific interview-based business podcasts, your message will be better received and you just might acquire more customers and fans along the way.

2

How Your Expert Status Attracts Podcast Hosts & Clients

So, why are you doing this?

You're reading this book because you're likely curious about the power of podcasts when it comes to marketing yourself and/or your business.

Is your goal to generate more revenue for your enterprise?

Is it to gain more exposure for you and your brand?

Is it to boost your email subscriber list numbers?

Is it to network with other professionals in your industry?

Whatever it is, get clear on it.

Prioritize what precise outcomes you're looking for that will make this marketing strategy worthwhile to you.

You can do this by simply writing them down in a list and numbering them in order from the most beneficial down to the least.

Once you have that clarity, you'll find your success will be easier to measure.

All of the above though is meaningless if you're not an expert in your niche and are not fantastic at what you do.

In today's world, it's never been easier to become an entrepreneur especially if you want to make your money online.

The barrier to entry is so low it seems like everyone is joining the party.

There's a problem with this.

Many of those party crashers arrive with nothing but sizzle and no substance.

Just take a look at your Instagram feed or check out a YouTube ad and notice all of those "Lifestyle Entrepreneurs" who are posing in front of mansions and fancy cars with promises that you can do the same if you buy what they're offering.

It's all a template and they're just following it step-by-step, but are they really experts or did they just borrow Dad's car without permission and pose with it in front of their rich Uncle Bradley's house when he wasn't home?

There are a lot of pretenders out there.

Sure, you can risk it and be one of them to make some quick cash, but once you're exposed then it's over until you hop onto the next trendy money-making opportunity.

That's not an expert.

That's not someone who can really help others.

You're better than that.

As an expert, you're a problem solver.

You want to be a credible one.

Once you are, you'll be more desirable to podcast hosts and will hopefully appear on their shows and provide great tips then you'll be taken seriously by their listeners who might buy your solutions to their problems.

Before you get there, you'll likely need to do some housekeeping.

Here's the thing.

When people hear you on a business podcast and find your content valuable, they will likely look you up online.

If you or your assistant reach out to podcast hosts, they'll Google you also.

So, it's pretty important that when they locate you that you're presenting a clear and authentic brand of who you are and what you provide.

There should be no confusion.

Before I get into that further, I'll give you an example of how crucial it is to make sure you have a strong online image.

This story features a real-life prospect for my podcast guest booking agency.

Get Booked!

Steve is a twenty-something fitness trainer from Toronto.

A really nice guy.

He would be an absolute dream to work with because he's laid back and would pay on time and would provide no headaches.

I knew him through mutual friends who referred him to me.

At the time, he provided his services to people in condos.

Like I said, Steve is a really awesome guy.

So, once I found out he was interested in my podcast guest booking services, I decided to look him up.

What I found online wasn't ideal.

It's not like he had anything obscene online, it's just his content was confusing, scattered and poorly produced.

He had multiple websites that featured different niches of his fitness training.

There were also terrible looking YouTube video testimonials Steve was a part of which promoted the self-help gurus whose events he had attended.

As for Steve's speaking himself, he was extremely stiff with little personality.

I thought to myself, "How can I sell him to podcast hosts?"

It saddened me because Steve is such a great person, but I knew if podcast hosts would research him, they'd find holes.

So, I had to have a tough phone call with him stating my thoughts and why I couldn't work with him.

To his credit, he took my constructive criticism very well.

If you're serious about appearing on business podcasts, you have to take control of your online presence and make some changes.

If you're wondering what podcast hosts and their guest bookers are looking for in a guest, here's some insight.

Since I've been a guest booker for 4 podcasts in my career (i.e.: The Stand Out NOW! Podcast, The

Successful Bookkeeper, The Thought Leader Revolution & The Breakdown with Dave & Audley basketball podcast), I ask myself these questions when evaluating potential guests.

1. Are they credible experts in their field?

2. Are they relevant to our audience?

3. Will they offer tips and suggestions that will help solve our listeners' problems?

4. Can they communicate clearly and effectively?

5. Will their personality work well with our host and will listeners like them?

6. Will they promote their interview to their email list in addition to their social media and personal networks?

7. Will they offer a free downloadable and useful gift to our audience?

To answer some of the above questions, I would…

- Check out their website
- Watch their YouTube videos

- Listen to their other podcast appearances and read any articles they've either written or appeared in regarding their niche
- Do a general online search to unearth any potential negative content about them

As you can see, your online presence matters.

To begin the process of your online renovation, here are some tips to consider.

Online Videos

- Delete any that are not relevant to your niche
- Remove any where you're not speaking clearly and are dressed poorly (i.e.: raggedy t-shirt, etc)
- Delete those where you're talking to the camera from an unprofessionally looking location (i.e.: someone's bathroom, etc)
- Delete any videos that are grainy, poorly lit and you're not using a microphone

Website

- Shut down all sites that don't focus on your target market

- Have one clean and uncluttered business site that clearly states in large text who you are and what product or service you provide (i.e.: Podcast Interview Experts – We Book Entrepreneurs Onto Interview-Based Business Podcasts)
- Display client testimonials and media appearances that will demonstrate you can do the job

Social Media

- Pick 1 to 2 social media websites that will be used to promote your business and connect with your prospects
- Keep your branding consistent through all of your channels including using the same logo and taglines
- Share your industry-based content with your followers consistently

All of the above will build your case when it comes to persuading podcast hosts that you're a valuable person to have on their show.

Remember, attempting to attract podcast hosts and potential clients is a dating process.

You need to prove yourself every step of the way and having your online presence under control will help you do that.

3

The Profitable Power of Business Podcasts & Where You Can Find Them

Where's the proof?

So far, you've read about how powerful podcast guest marketing can be, but you haven't seen any evidence.

Until now.

Let me tell you a story about a person I've coached when it comes to booking business podcast appearances.

His name is Michael Palmer.

Dave Mendonca

He's a 40-something year old part owner of a bookkeeping business training and development company called Pure Bookkeeping North America……

…and he's the host of The Successful Bookkeeper podcast.

He leads the Canadian arm of Pure Bookkeeping while its headquarters are based in Australia.

Pure Bookkeeping North America serves American and Canadian bookkeeping business owners by offering them a proven plug and play system of various Sales & Marketing, Human Resources and Bookkeeping standard operating procedures that licensees would follow like a recipe book and implement into their businesses.

After much research (i.e.: prospect surveys, analyzing demographics of current clients, etc), he has figured out that his niche is 35-54 year old American female bookkeeping business owners, who are overworked, underpaid and underappreciated, with families.

If you're not familiar with the bookkeeping industry, which I wasn't since before meeting Palmer, bookkeepers are considered invisible when compared to accountants who usually receive more of the respect and spotlight when working with entrepreneurs and their businesses.

With all this specific information about his niche at his disposal, Palmer wanted to start appearing on relevant podcasts to spread the word about Pure Bookkeeping.

After some research, he booked an appearance on the following show...

The above podcast is listened to by accountants and bookkeepers.

You can check out Palmer's appearance below:

Grow My Accounting Practice

https://www.profitfirstprofessionals.com/2017/07/27/operating-procedures-can-drive-business-forward-michael-palmer-ep-106/

As a result of focusing on a podcast that Palmer's bookkeeper audience liked, magical things started to happen.

Bookkeepers were reaching out to him about buying the Pure Bookkeeping System.

Here is a sample web form that Jeannie filled out before speaking with Palmer.

First Name	Jeannie
Commitment?	10
3-4 Hours a week?	Yes
What part of the Pure Bookkeeping System are you most looking forward to?	the marketing side
How did you hear about the Pure Bookkeeping System?	**gmap podcast**

She discovered Pure Bookkeeping after hearing Palmer on the Grow My Accounting Practice (GMAP) Podcast and would buy the Pure Bookkeeping System.

Palmer made thousands of dollars by appearing ONE TIME on the GMAP podcast where he gave the audience valuable tips.

As long as GMAP is alive, his interview will continue to be listened to by new people over and over again which can lead to more sales.

To further prove this marketing strategy works, I booked guests onto Palmer's Successful Bookkeeper podcast including GMAP podcast host and the author of *Profit First*, Mike Michalowicz.

You can listen to his appearance at the below link.

https://www.thesuccessfulbookkeeper.com/episodes/24

After Michalowicz delivered some useful information to the bookkeeper audience, Palmer received this email from one of his Pure Bookkeeping licensees.

---------- Forwarded message ----------

From: **Virginia**

Date: Sun, Jul 16, 2017 at 6:13 PM

Subject: Thank you!

To: michael@purebookkeeping.ca

Hello Michael,

I wanted to thank you for all that you and your company are doing for the bookkeepers in Canada and around the world.

I am a big fan of The Successful Bookkeeper Podcast and was so happy to have found this at the perfect time for me. I have started my own business after working as a bookkeeper for 2 years and previously being a small business owner about 6 years ago in BC.

The Successful Bookkeeper was the first of the Facebook bookkeeping communities that I joined. **Since then I have listened to all the episodes and particularly enjoyed the one with Mike Michalowicz and about his book Profit First. After hearing this I bought that book and I am now a Profit First Professional working my way through the training program.**

Thank you again for all that you do and I look forward to meeting you one day out and about in the bookkeeping community.

Virginia

She became a client of Mike Michalowicz.

Palmer's Successful Bookkeeper podcast doesn't have a giant audience.

It averages over 7000 downloads per month, but it's the concentration of the bookkeeper niche which proved profitable for Michalowicz.

He and Palmer's successful interviews are exactly what can happen when you know your audience, appear on podcasts that are filled with your ideal clients and deliver useful information to help them solve their problems.

So, where can you find your suitable business podcasts?

Since you should have a good idea of your client avatar by now, I'll provide some links to websites that will have podcast databases for you to review.

Before I do, here are a few tips to keep in mind when doing your research.

1. Google podcasts that feature keywords in their website titles and content descriptions that are related to your niche.

For example with Michael Palmer, he'd look for shows that mentioned bookkeepers.

He could search "bookkeeper podcasts" and see what results would be provided.

2. Investigate what podcasts other experts in your niche have appeared on as guests.

Since they've already been there, they've vetted the show to make sure it's worth their time.

Visit the websites of these experts and look in their media sections to see their past podcast interviews.

Be careful though, you don't want to pitch these podcasts too close to when other similar experts have appeared on them.

Give it a few months before reaching out.

3. If you located a podcast you like, be sure to listen to past episodes to make sure the host and content are a fit for you.

You don't want to appear on a show you didn't pre-listen to then you're on the podcast and all of a sudden the host swears and screams into the microphone while interviewing you.

Avoid this by listening to the show before pitching the host!

4. Don't be distracted by massive podcast download numbers.

Many entrepreneurs seem to think they need to appear on The Tim Ferriss Show or some other widely popular podcast that has hundreds of millions of downloads to make it a profitable experience for them.

That's not always the case.

I've discovered in my podcast guest booking career that clients have found success when they appear on podcasts that have lower download numbers, but their audiences are filled with their ideal prospects.

Appearing on mainstream podcasts may not attract the specific clients you're looking for, so don't dismiss smaller niche shows.

5. Ask your current clients what podcasts they listen to.

Chances are if your customers are listening to certain shows, there may be future clients who are as well.

Hopefully those tips will be of help.

As promised, here are some websites to find interview-based business podcasts.

iTunes

https://itunes.apple.com/ca/genre/podcasts-business/id1321?mt=2

Stitcher

https://www.stitcher.com/stitcher-list/business-and-industry-podcasts-top-shows

Podbean

https://www.podbean.com/business-podcasts

PlayerFM

https://player.fm/featured/business

BlogTalkRadio

http://www.blogtalkradio.com/business

Listen Notes Podcast Search Engine

https://www.listennotes.com/search/?q=business&sort_by_date=0&scope=episode&offset=0&language=Any%20language&len_min=0

Of course, those aren't the only places to find podcasts.

I reached out to some business podcast stars to see where they look to secure appearances and here's what they had to say.

John Lee Dumas, the host of the hit business podcast, Entrepreneurs On Fire, explains, "Sometimes recommendations, sometimes through the podcaster reaching out to me with a request to be on their show, and sometimes by doing research in iTunes – typing in keywords that match up with the topics I know I can speak to."

And New York Times best-selling author and host of The School of Greatness podcast, Lewis Howes says, "I'm always looking at the iTunes charts and on social media at who's doing what, what's getting noticed, what shows people are talking about."

As you can tell, there are plenty of options out there.

After coming up with a list of 5-10 podcasts you think are a fit, now it's time to get your pitch together.

4

The Pitch Email: Your Ticket To The Show

Your inbox is a daily battlefield.

Marketers, corporations, media, thought leaders, charities, retailers, vendors, clients and so on, are all pushing and shoving each other for the chance to earn a second of your time.

For an email, especially a cold one, to grab your attention enough to actually open it, can be a major victory for the person who sent it.

The thing you probably don't realize is there's a lot of psychology that goes into crafting an email, including an eye-catching subject line, that is persuasive enough to move you to action.

I'll get to that in few minutes.

Before I do, why are pitch emails so important?

Well, they are an opportunity to present your best case to a podcast host as to why you should be on her show without having to worry about a gatekeeper hanging up on you.

Emails are easier and less creepy then making cold phone calls to strangers plus you can deliver them whenever you want.

However, I do recommend if you send pitch emails that you ship them before 9am on the day you'd like, so that your message is at the top of host's inbox.

Of course it won't mean a thing if your pitch email isn't good.

In this chapter, you'll be equipped to not only stand out, but you'll be able to present such a compelling case via email that podcast hosts will have no other choice but to book you on their shows.

You're about to witness a step-by-step analysis of what makes an irresistible podcast pitch email that actually works.

Some of the principles you will learn have enabled me to book clients onto interview-based business podcasts that have attracted new customers and business relationships.

As well, throughout my media career, I've used a few of these secrets, to secure podcast guests such as New York Times best-selling author, Seth Godin, Shark Tank TV star, Barbara Corcoran and Supermodel turned Business Mogul, Kathy Ireland in addition to arranging print interviews with celebrities such as Grammy Award-winner, Beyoncé Knowles and Star Wars actor, Anthony "C-3PO" Daniels to name a few.

With that in mind, now let's begin.

1) Shatter The Inbox Noise With A Compelling Subject Line Title

Do me a favor?

Login to your email and check out all of your new and old messages then take a look at the emails in your trash bin.

Of the emails you saw, which ones did you actually read because of pure interest and which others did you send to the fiery depths of your waste bin for eternity?

What was the difference between both types of emails?

Odds are it was likely the subject line that was the game changer.

When pitching podcast hosts and producers, especially those who are connected to popular shows, you have to remember they receive guest requests all the time, so your subject line has to POP.

Here are a few types that could get you past the front door.

The Mutual Reference Hook

Obviously, before sending cold pitch emails, identify first if you have any mutual connections with the podcast host.

If you do, it'll be a much easier and quicker road.

Investigate if you share any mutual friends, colleagues and family.

You can do this by…

i) **Visiting her social media networks**

ii) **Viewing her podcast guest list to see if you know anybody**

iii) **Reading her blog, website & books for any mentions**

If there is a connection, reach out to that person and ask if you can use her name when contacting the podcast host.

Of course, when asking this favor make sure you offer something in return that is interesting to that person.

Once you receive approval, here's a sample Mutual Reference subject line template you can use.

Hi (Podcast Host First Name), (Mutual Reference Full Name) Referred Me To You...

This line is intriguing because you're mentioning a person the host knows in some way who hopefully she likes and trusts and is curious to find out more about what the email is about.

The Geography Hook

Since I'm based in Canada, I use this novelty when pitching US business podcasts and it works. For many American hosts, they might think it's refreshing or surprising that someone from another country is interested in their show.

It can be flattering knowing that your podcast is picking up traction beyond your borders.

For example, a subject line could be...

Hi Jenny, Greetings From Toronto! A Podcast Guest Idea For You...

So, let's breakdown that subject line.

a) **Hi Jenny** - It's important to personalize all of your subject lines otherwise podcast hosts and guest bookers will likely think your email is spam.

b) **Greetings from Toronto!** - Using the word "Greetings" is a nice way of introducing yourself to a stranger then when you add "Toronto" that taps into the uniqueness of someone outside of your country taking the time to reach out to you because of her interest in your podcast.

c) **A Podcast Guest Idea For You** - This briefly explains why you're visiting in the first place. I'll comment more on this in a moment.

The Geography hook is effective when...

- Both you and the podcast host or guest booker you're pitching are located in cities that are far from each other. If you're based in Manhattan and the host you're contacting is in Brooklyn, she will probably think, "who cares?" If you're based in Egypt then you reach out to the Brooklyn-based podcaster, she will likely be impressed.

- The host is from your country but mainly receives guest pitches from other countries. For example, when I guest booked for The Thought Leader Revolution podcast (formerly The Business of Thought Leadership), I pitched Toronto native, Jon Nastor of The Hack The Entrepreneur podcast and he said, "Hey Dave, Thanks for reaching out. I'm responding from Toronto, so you got me with the subject line!"

For Jon, since his main audience is likely outside of Canada, he was probably used to hearing from Americans and others that weren't Canadian, so when he saw Toronto in the subject line, it was relatable to him and created instant rapport. As a result, he would read my email then later on, I'd book a guest on his podcast.

The "Podcast Guest Idea For You" Hook

It's effective because it's personalized, gets to the point and offers help to the podcast host or guest booker.

A sample subject line could be…

Hi Jenny, A Podcast Guest Idea For You...

Notice that there's no mention of the podcast guest's name. That's to create curiosity so a podcast host or guest booker would want to find out more.

The "Trade Podcast Interviews" Hook

If you already host an interview-based business podcast, you can leverage your platform by offering a spot on your show in exchange for one on the podcast you'd like to appear on.

This hook only works if the podcast host you're contacting sees value in being on your show.

She normally can determine if it's worth her time by…

- How many notable guests you've had on your podcast
- The number of downloads your show receives
- Whether your podcast suits her target audience

A sample subject line could be...

Hi Jenny, Podcast Guest Appearance Trade...

That subject line will spark some curiosity which will motivate the podcast host to click your email.

Since you now have some subject line options to explore, let's take a look at the ingredients of a persuasive email to a podcast host or guest booker.

2) Be Nice & Introduce Yourself

This is where a friendly greeting goes a long way.

Here's a sample...

Hi Jenny,

I trust you had a good weekend. My name is Dave Mendonca. I'm a podcast guest booker from Podcast Interview Experts.

It's pretty self-explanatory. Be polite. Ask how the podcast host or guest booker are doing then mention your name and job title or how you're relevant to the host.

3) Acknowledge The Host's Time

You're not the only one contacting podcast hosts or guest bookers to be on their shows.

They don't have time to deal with inconsiderate people, so in order to get on their good side, here's an optional sentence that will make them feel like you're a good person and they will likely reward you by continuing to read your email.

I apologize for visiting completely out of the blue. I realize you're extremely busy, so I'll be quick.

You'd be surprised how disarming being nice and respectful can be.

I like putting this sentence in the email so the host or guest booker realizes that I understand and respect their time is precious, but what I'm going to mention will be quick and valuable.

You're looking out for them.

Chances are because of how nice you are, the host or guest booker will like you enough to continue reading.

You're building that trust and rapport which is crucial to moving them to further action.

4) Ask For The Interview

Now, you get to the point and ask for the interview as briefly as you can.

Here's an example…

I'd like to add to the quality of your (insert podcast name) podcast by asking if you'd be interested in having (insert guest name) on your show?

For those who are trying to book themselves on a podcast, I realize the above question may feel a little awkward because you'd rather have someone else ask for you instead of potentially looking desperate.

Let go of that mindset.

In 2015, I secured an entire media book tour (complete with TV, radio, blog, print and podcast appearances) by myself for my first traditional published book,

100 Things Raptors Fans Should Know & Do Before They Die.

If I felt weird about it, there was no way I could book those media opportunities.

Forget what others think and focus on what your podcast appearances will ultimately do for you and your business.

In the above example, I used the word "quality" because you do want to compliment the show.

The host probably invests a lot of time into making her podcast great, so respect that by mentioning some well-deserved kudos.

5) Your Credibility

So, you've made the ask, but why should the podcast host consider you when he doesn't even know your credentials?

This is the part of the email when you serve up that information.

Here's an example...

I'm a trusted branding expert who is an in-demand speaker for clients such as Google and Microsoft and I'm a New York Times best-selling author.

Again, you want your bio to communicate your credentials and expertise in a tight sentence or two.

Discuss your relevant titles, skills, connections and accomplishments that back up why you're an ideal choice to be on the show.

6) Your Picture

What I like to do within pitch emails is insert or copy and paste a picture of the person I'm booking.

Why?

I find the picture helps with building rapport and making it a more personal experience for the podcast host.

If you see a pleasant face, you're likely to give that person more of your attention.

Is having a picture a must? No, it isn't.

I've sent pitch emails without pictures and still secured bookings, so it's optional.

If you decide to include a picture, here are some tips.

a) Make sure it's a headshot from the chest up.

b) Dress business casual or business formal or whatever you feel is appropriate for the podcast host you're contacting.

c) Make sure you pose in front of a plain background with nothing distracting around you.

d) Take the picture with a high quality camera or smartphone and make sure the picture is high resolution.

e) SMILE! Everyone responds well to someone who looks happy.

f) One more thing, make sure your picture is NOT a selfie.

You want it to look professional and not amateur, but still communicating a sense of friendliness that would endear a podcast host.

7) The Golden Nuggets You'll Provide

This part of the email is crucial.

This is where you prove your value to the podcast host.

She doesn't want somebody who will be a shameless promoter on her show.

If you don't bring helpful tips, knowledge and insight to the host's audience, she will likely shut you down.

So, how do you figure out what's valuable to her listeners?

Do your research by actually listening to an episode or two to get a feel for the content.

When you check out the podcast, take a peek at its website, evaluate what skills, knowledge or tips you have that would align with the content of that show.

Make sure when you're thinking of your points that your tips haven't been covered in past episodes.

Usually on the podcast website, you'll be able to go back and see what has been previously published.

When you're deciding on your tips, make sure to come up with 3 of them.

In my experience, having 3 concise points featuring your suggestions is very effective because the brain finds it relatively easy to grasp threes.

When crafting the 3 points make sure they're written in a how-to or instructive kind of way.

For example…

Jenny will provide great value to your audience by discussing...

- **How to create your brand from scratch even if you don't have time**
- **Why you should leverage the power of Facebook Ads to promote yourself**
- **Why speaking at industry conferences is a must to building your network**

Once you nail these down, it will resonate with the podcast host and eventually it will interest the listeners when you discuss those topics on the show.

The great thing is if you're not receiving any podcast bites, you can always tweak those bullet points to make them more relevant to the next show you contact.

8) Have A Bonus For The Audience

At this point, you've introduced yourself, stated your request, illustrated what valuable tips you can bring to the podcast, but if you really want to sweeten things, provide a free download or product or discount on a service that would be relevant and useful for the audience.

Everybody loves free stuff!

So, see what goodies you can offer.

Here's a sample...

She'd love to give you a couple of her branding books for free, so you can give them away to your listeners.

Utilize the law of reciprocity which, according to social psychologists, basically means when someone does something nice for you, there's a deep-rooted psychological urge within you to do something nice in return.

So, offer gifts then see where it takes you.

9) Reinforce Your Credibility

Yes, you've already stated your bio, but here's where you can add extra weight by providing links to your previous podcast, television and radio interviews.

This is important, so the host can find out how you verbally communicate.

Whatever links you provide make sure they have your best content.

If you have appearances from major media outlets this is where you include them.

As well, you can type in links to your website, articles, testimonials from notable people that would impress the podcast host or anything else that is relevant and that makes you more credible.

Here's an example of what you can say…

If you'd like more information on Jenny, visit this link – https://www.ILoveBranding.com.

To hear her appearance on The Branding Experts podcast, listen here – https://brandingexpertspodcast.com/jenny.

To watch her Today Show appearance, click here – https://www.today.com/jenny/.

10) Look Forward, Give Thanks & Sign Off

This is pretty straightforward.

Just mention to the podcast host or guest booker you look forward to their thoughts and thank them for their time.

Once you do that, sign off by saying anything like "Best regards", "Have a great day!", "Enjoy your night!"

Here's an example….

I look forward to your thoughts.

Thank you for your time.

Best regards,

11) Your Sign Off Email Signature

In one last bit of credibility, if you have a decent looking logo in your email signature, it will make you look more professional.

It sends the message that you've invested in your business and take things seriously.

For example…

Dave Mendonca

Founder, Podcast Interview Experts

http://www.PodcastInterviewExperts.com

416- 555-1212

Within your email signature make sure to include your name, title, website link, email address and phone number.

Your Pitch Email

After going through all of the previous steps, here's a sample of what your final pitch email could look like.

Subject title: Hi ___, A Podcast Guest Idea For You...

Hello _____,

I trust all is well.

My name is _____. I'm a _____ .

I apologize for visiting completely out of the blue. I realize you're extremely busy, so I'll be quick.

I'd like to add to the quality of your _____ podcast by asking if you'd be interested in having me on your show?

I'm a trusted expert in _____and author of _____.

I will provide great value to your audience by discussing...

- How to _____

- How to _____

- How to _____

I would like to offer a free _____ for your listeners.

To find out more about me, click here (insert website link).

To listen and/or watch my past media appearances, view below. (insert links of past podcast, radio & TV interviews)

I look forward to your thoughts.

Thank you for your time.

Best regards,

(Insert Your Name)

(Insert Your Title & Company Name)

(Insert Your Website Link)

(Insert Your Phone Number)

(Insert Your Company Logo)

The Glory Is In The Follow Up

Here's the reality.

You may splash inboxes from coast-to-coast, but you might not hear from podcast hosts or guest bookers right away.

Don't panic.

You just need to follow up two days after your original email.

Here's a sample message you can use.

Subject line: Hi ___, Follow Up…Re: Hi ___, A Podcast Guest Idea For You…

Hi ____,

I trust all is well.

My name is _____.

I'm visiting to find out if you received my recent email and what your thoughts are regarding it.

I look forward to your response.

Thank you for your time.

Best regards,

Dave

Another follow up subject line I've found effective in the past is…

Hi ___, Confirmation…Re: Hi ___, A Podcast Guest Idea For You…

There's something about the word "confirmation" that piques curiosity.

If you still don't hear from the podcast host, wait another two days and send the below email.

Subject line: URGENT! Hi ___, Your Thoughts? …Hi ___, Follow UP…Re: Hi ____, A Podcast Guest Idea For You…

Hi ___,

I trust all is well.

I wanted to stop by to make sure you've been receiving my emails.

I look forward to your thoughts.

Thank you for your time.

Best regards,

Dave

So, you might ask why I included all 3 previous subject lines…

URGENT! Hi ___, Your Thoughts?...Re: Hi ___, Follow UP…Re: Hi ___, A Podcast Guest Idea For You…

I leave them just in case the podcast host needs a reminder of your request.

If you still don't hear anything, there's a good chance the host or guest booker are not interested or you have the wrong email address or there's some other factor that is preventing a response.

If the host or guest booker do finally email you back, but says you're not a fit, be professional and polite by thanking them for their consideration and time then wish them well.

However, if you do receive a positive response to your follow up or urgent emails, go ahead and ask for what dates and times the podcast host can do an interview.

It's all about persistence.

Just keep sending out those pitch emails and follow them up then eventually you'll receive the breakthrough you're looking for.

5

You've Booked The Podcast Interview, NOW WHAT?

Congratulations!

If you followed the directions from the previous chapters, you might have secured an appearance on an interview-based business podcast in your niche by now.

If you did, your real work has only just begun.

Before going on a podcast, it's important to have a game plan, so you can have clear objectives about what you'd like to achieve.

Remember, being on a show that gives you a direct channel to speak to your ideal customers is a great opportunity.

Don't blow it.

You can do this by understanding that your focus during your podcast appearance should be the following ...

1) **To offer valuable tips and resources to the audience**
2) **To make the podcast host look good and be useful to her**
3) **To giveaway a free downloadable product or offer a discounted service**

Let's breakdown the reasons behind these choices.

Why is it important to offer valuable tips and resources to a podcast audience?

Some might ask, "Why can't I just go on a podcast to promote my stuff? I see big celebrities go on television talk shows all the time to discuss their projects without giving any sort of advice to the audience, so why can't I do the same for my business or brand?"

Well, first off, no offense, but you're most likely not a big time celebrity.

Secondly, interview-based business podcasts are more educational in nature.

Typically, listeners don't consume those shows hoping to hear sales pitches. They're looking for tactical strategies, tips, suggestions and shortcuts to solve the annoying issues in their businesses and lives.

They mostly don't care about who you are, but they do pay attention if you have the solutions to their painful problems.

So, always think about how you can help listeners FIRST before delivering a sales pitch.

And don't worry, normally, the host will give you an opportunity to promote at the end of the podcast after you've provided great content for her audience.

Why should I make the podcast host look good? What do you mean I have to be useful to her?

You have to realize the podcast host has put in a lot of hard work, time and financial resources into building her show to a point where she can attract a good-sized audience.

Her listeners trust she'll provide quality episodes that will serve their needs and look out for them.

So, if she picks a guest who isn't a fit, she's in jeopardy of breaking that trust and losing her listeners.

If that happens, that could mean losing advertising revenue, fewer clients for her business outside of the show and bad publicity online.

This is why it's extremely important that she chooses her guests wisely.

Some of the ways you can make her look good in front of her listeners is by...

a) **Being a credible expert in your niche and being ready to present insightful stories and useful content that are relevant, entertaining and helpful to the audience**
b) **Having a good attitude and enjoying the conversation with no hint of being snarky, narcissistic, negatively sarcastic or condescending towards the host and audience**

c) Offering free and valuable stuff that positively impacts her listeners

In regards to ways you can be useful to the host, here's one that you probably don't hear much about.

I remember having a chat with a business podcast host who mentioned his guests receive more value from his curated audience than he does from the guest himself.

Many of the hosts of interview-based business podcasts are entrepreneurs themselves.

They're trying to make a living, so if you find ways to either bring them clients directly or even sales leads as a part of your deal that can be useful to them.

Another option is actually paying for your spot on a show.

Personally, I'm not fan of this route because I feel you could get booked onto great business podcasts for FREE that are targeted towards your niche which would provide you more sales leads than spending money on a massively popular business podcast that hits more of a broader audience.

So, do your best to bring some sort of financial value to the podcast host even if it's you, at the very least, marketing her business to your network or connecting her with powerful influencers in her niche that she can have conversations with.

Those connections could lead to great opportunities for her which could lead to return appearances on her podcast for you.

Why should I giveaway a free downloadable product or a discounted service?

When you're a guest at someone's house, especially, a person you just met, do you bring a gift, wine or food to give as a token of thanks for the invite? Well, you should because that's the etiquette that works well with podcast hosts and their listeners.

If you give a free, valuable and downloadable gift (i.e.: a checklist, e-book, report, etc.) or a discounted service that is relevant to that audience, you'll give it something useful immediately, so it'll make the host look great then she'll likely want you back. Win-Win-Win.

Not only that, you can use that gift or discounted service as an opt-in into your email list because you'll provide a link that sends people to your website where your opt-in box or form resides then they'll enter their email address to access the download or information about how to obtain the discounted service.

This is massive because once you have people in your email list and you nurture them with great free content and value, they'll like and trust you enough that you can send them future offers to buy your products and services and now they'll be more open to purchasing them.

This is a huge piece of how you can generate revenue through your podcast appearances.

Ask The Host For Questions

Another way to prepare for your interview is to email the podcast host or guest booker to see if they have any idea what questions the host will ask during the show.

If the host prefers an organic conversation, she might not give you the questions in fear that the interview may sound rehearsed.

If that's the case, ask for the topic that will be covered then try to anticipate what questions may be asked.

You can also check out past interviews of that podcast to see if the host had similar guests as you to get a gauge of what she might ask.

Obviously, she likely won't give you the same questions, but it might be a good frame of reference.

Have Great Audio

Of course, when it comes to preparing for your interview, you have to make sure you have quality audio.

Back when I first co-hosted a basketball podcast called The Breakdown with Dave & Audley from 2008-2013, my partner, Audley Stephenson and I used BlogTalkRadio.com as our platform to interview people.

We conducted these conversations strictly through our cell phones.

When I listen back to those interviews, the audio was just terrible.

Today's podcast listener doesn't tolerate poor audio and that's the same for podcast hosts.

So, as a guest, you better make sure you sound great.

How do you do this?

Here a few suggestions:

1) Have a decent microphone

You don't need a high end one to start.

Just a mic that you can plug into your laptop that does the job.

The one I use is very affordable, works well with any recording software and it comes with its own mic stand and has given me no problems.

It's called the Audio-Technica ATR2100-USB Cardiod Dynamic USB/XLR Microphone.

You can learn more about it below -

https://www.amazon.com/Audio-Technica-ATR2100-USB-Cardioid-Dynamic-Microphone/dp/B004QJOZS4

To look for more microphone options and information on other related podcast equipment, John Lee Dumas has a great comprehensive list you can check out at this link.

https://www.eofire.com/podcastequipment/

2) Be in a quiet room

When you're doing an interview, make sure there are no distractions or interruptions.

Close the door.

Turn off your phone, notifications and any other device that makes noise.

Make sure your pets, kids and spouse/significant other do not enter the room.

If you're going to have clear audio, there can't be any background noise.

3) Have a Skype account

Many business podcast hosts will use Skype to call you and record their interviews.

Skype's audio quality is pretty clean and a big improvement over talking over a landline phone.

If you have Skype, the host can call you directly for no charge to either of you.

If you don't have Skype, the host will need to buy credits to call you.

To sign up for your free Skype account, check out this link - https://www.skype.com/.

Some podcast hosts also use Zoom which is a video and web conferencing service that has good audio as well.

To learn more about it, visit here - https://zoom.us.

Alright, your pre-interview preparation is all set.

Now, it's time to figure out how you can handle the spotlight.

6

How To Ace Your Podcast Interview

Welcome to interview day.

All your preparation has led up to this moment.

But, before you jump on the call, there are some last minute things to do.

1 - On the day of your interview, email or contact the podcast host to have a quick pre-interview conversation

See if she can call you 10 minutes earlier to discuss the interview game plan and also to test your microphone.

If you don't hear from the host, just call 10 minutes earlier anyway to see if you can catch her.

2 - Get a glass of water

During the interview, your voice may get dry, so you'll need a refreshment on hand.

3 - Go to the bathroom

It's not a good look if you have to go for a pee break in the middle of the interview.

4 - Warm up your voice

A good way to loosen your jaw and heat up your vocal chords is to simply annunciate the letters "A-E-I-O-U" repeatedly 5-10 times and do so by opening your mouth as wide as you can.

I learned this exercise back in my Radio Broadcasting college program days.

5 - Make sure your door is closed

Double check that there won't be any interruptions or distractions and shut the door.

How Do You Handle Nervousness?

Whether it's your first podcast appearance or your 50th, you may be nervous.

It's a good thing because it means you care about the outcome.

Another one of the reasons it's great to have a pre-interview with the host is to get more comfortable with her and to develop rapport which will ease your nerves.

Remember, no matter how popular that podcast host is, she's still just a human being like you, so don't psyche yourself out.

When you're being interviewed, make sure you're just focused on the host.

It's a conversation between you and her.

Forget the microphone and the possibility that thousands of people could listen to your interview.

Just concentrate on having the most authentic conversation with that person.

Listeners will resonate with that.

It's okay to be nervous, but there are ways to handle it, so it doesn't have to derail your performance.

What's Your Story?

You see, acing your business podcast interview can have many ingredients.

During your interview, the use of storytelling can be a terrific tool.

It has been around since the dawn of humankind. It's lasted this long because it continues to be a great way to captivate people. It's especially powerful when you're authentic.

"Lead with vulnerability," Howes recommends. "That's what creates connection with an audience. Talk about your failures, the things you learned when you made mistakes, the times when you didn't have it all figured out. That's what people connect to."

Beth Buelow, the author of *The Introvert Entrepreneur*, agrees.

"People buy from people, and when you're in conversation and sharing your stories, you're connecting in a deeper way with potential clients and customers. They feel like they know you after listening to you and hearing the passion in your voice. And for most interviews, you get to talk about your business without pitching – it's more about who you are, why you do what you do and what's important about it. You're putting know, like and trust before the pitch, as it should be!"

She adds, "My goal is to provide three things. Solid information that's gleaned from a combination of research, reflection, personal experience and training; questions for the listener to reflect on; and tips to support them in taking action."

Another little tip to building rapport with the podcast host is -- use her first name all the time.

It's a nice little touch that goes unnoticed a lot these days.

It shows you have respect for that person and she'll respond well to that.

Humor

During your interview, it doesn't hurt if you have a sense of humor. You don't need to be serious all the time.

You're on the podcast to share your expertise with listeners, so there's no need to feel pressure because you're doing your best to help people.

You can lighten up.

If you have a sense of humor that allows you to have more of a personality then the audience receives not only useful tips, but an entertaining episode as well.

7

How To Attract Sales Leads From Your Podcast Appearance

Finally!

How do you actually make money from appearing on interview-based business podcasts?

As I revealed earlier with the Michael Palmer and Michael Michalowicz examples, the ability to make thousands to hundreds of thousands of dollars via your podcast interviews is definitely possible.

To recap, here's what helped Palmer and Michalowicz attract clients through their podcast appearances.

1 - They were experts in their niche who really knew their stuff

2 - They provided the podcast audience with valuable and relevant tips

3 - They offered useful, free and downloadable gifts with strong calls to action to guide listeners to their websites which ultimately lead to an email opt-in area

Your Call To Action

Once you provide your golden nuggets of information and you've built trust with the listener, the key move is to provide an irresistible call to action.

You're hoping that you've created enough interest that people will want to engage with you beyond the interview.

"Because when you deliver high value to an audience who you know wants and needs that value, there's really no reason for them not to check out your business and what you have going on," Dumas says. "I always end my guest appearances with a strong call to action, which rarely has anything to do with selling anything. Typically

I'm just sharing a free resource available on our site so I can start nurturing a relationship with the new leads."

Dumas also mentioned a good call to action could be sharing your email address or asking people to connect with you via your favorite social platform.

Typically though, you want to guide people to an email opt-in area, so you can add them as a subscriber.

How To Make Money Off Your Email List

Why is having one so important?

Well, it's your direct channel to communicating with your ideal audience.

Once people have given you their email address, they're giving you the permission and honor of staying in direct communication with them.

Advertisers would kill to have that kind of access.

But, this is something not to take lightly.

Don't be that slimy salesperson who is so desperate to cash in that you spam your email subscribers to death.

That won't go over well.

Instead, these people are trusting you to provide them continuous value in the form of useful content, relevant industry news updates and offers to buy products that will enhance their businesses and lives.

Once you keep giving them great content then the once in a while announcement that you have an exciting new product that could solve their problems will actually be noticed and purchased.

The relationship with your email subscribers is like any relationship that is starting out where you're always trying to build trust and rapport to the point that people feel safe to work with you and eventually support you.

Another reason why email lists are so powerful is it's your captive audience.

What if Facebook or LinkedIn or your other social media network of choice were to disappear forever, there goes all of your contacts that you worked hard to acquire.

With social media, you don't own those platforms, but you do own your email list.

No bankruptcy or company take over will harm that.

So, there's some security there.

Once your email subscribers continue to see you're authentically trying to help solve their problems, they will buy your stuff when it's relevant to them.

The thing is, you don't even need an email list that features over a 100,000 email addresses to make money.

I know one entrepreneur who has an email list of just over 1000 and he's already made thousands of dollars off that list.

One of the keys for him is he has a niche audience and he caters to those people with specific content and offers that he knows they'll be interested in.

What If I Don't Want To Do The Content Long Game?

If you're on an interview-based business podcast and you'd like to promote an offer directly, without the long game of having people join your email list then you delivering them valuable content then ultimately presenting them offers, it is possible.

At the end of your interview, you can just tell people briefly about your offer and why it can help them then direct them to a website page where they can buy the product directly.

To go a step further, if you're selling a book and you want people to buy it right away, you can direct them to your website, but also think about offering some free sample chapters as added incentive which could make them want to purchase your book more quickly.

If you're not going to give your product or service for free, I'd recommend offering a discount using a promo code.

You can track promo codes, but it would be ideal if you can also have people join your email list too, so you have them in your ecosystem.

What Downloadable Products Can I Offer?

It really doesn't have to be complicated.

A free download could easily be a checklist of **What To Do or Not To Do** in regards to something in your niche.

For example, **10 Things Bookkeepers Shouldn't Say To Their Clients.**

It just has to be valuable and easy to read for people.

You just type that content into a word document then save it as a PDF then create a webpage for it explaining what is and how it can help its target audience.

You include an email opt-in box on the site then when people visit and opt-in, you send them the PDF.

Ideally, that's how it should work.

To see a good example of a website that offers a free download, visit the following link.

https://www.digitalmarketer.com/lp/fb-ad-templates/

In addition to checklists, you can create small e-books, sample chapters and templates to name a few.

How Do I Create & Manage My Email List?

There are many different options out there which house your email list and allow you to automate your marketing messages any day or time you'd like.

You can go the mostly free route by using Mail Chimp.

https://mailchimp.com

Or you can get more advanced and pricey with software such as…

Get Booked!

Infusionsoft - https://www.infusionsoft.com

ConvertKit - https://convertkit.com

AWeber - https://www.aweber.com

Of course, there are many more choices out there, but the above list is a good start.

If you'd like to follow an email list expert who has tons of free resources and is a proven rock star in her field, I recommend Amy Porterfield.

I've had the great pleasure of interviewing her for Entrepreneur.com and she really knows her stuff.

You can check out her content at:

https://www.amyporterfield.com and listen to her Online Marketing Made Easy podcast at this link.

https://www.amyporterfield.com/amy-porterfield-podcast/

As Amy probably knows, if, as a business podcast guest, you can have an irresistible call to action coupled with a great free download and system to capture and nurture email subscribers, before you know it, sales leads and clients will be flooding your inbox.

8

Generate Opportunities Beyond The Interview

Your podcast appearance is just the beginning.

Yes, it can lead to sales leads and potential clients from podcast listeners, but you're forgetting somebody – the podcast host.

By being on that person's show, you're entering into her network.

This is one of the reasons why it's so crucial you leave a good impression.

Earlier, we covered the importance of making sure you bring something of value to the podcast host whether it be prospects, actual clients for her business or at the very least an introduction to industry influencers.

Before, during and after that interview, it's a chance to build a connection with her.

By doing this, who knows what kind of opportunities you could attract if she likes you enough to become your ally?

Once the interview is done, usually, you'll have a minute or two to speak with the podcast host.

During that time, be sure to thank the podcast host for having you on and let her know how appreciative you are for the opportunity.

As well, mention if there's any way you can be of help to her that she should not hesitate in contacting you.

After ending the call, be sure to email the host a thank you that same day and let her know you had a great time and that you're around if she ever needs your support.

You don't want to come off as too needy or desperate.

Just be classy and respectful.

Eventual Millionaire author and podcast host, Jaime Masters, who interviews millionaires for her show, has some ideas on how you can further the connection beyond the podcast interview.

"I try to follow up with something helpful, such as a referral to someone they want to meet or sending a prospect their way or something to give them. I've even sent pizza socks to one of them because we were joking about pizza socks for some reason on the podcast."

Before, during and after the interview, always pay attention when the host gives you a window into her likes and hobbies.

Who knows? You may have some of them in common and can leverage that in the future.

Some other suggestions to connect beyond the interview can be...

- **You can ask if the podcast host is interested in a meetup for a coffee or meal if she's ever visiting your hometown or vice versa**
- **You could reach out to the podcast host before an upcoming conference and suggest a meetup if she's going too**
- **If she has a new book or program launching, have her as a guest on your podcast, if you have one**

It's always important to be valuable to the podcast host even after the interview.

If you're serious about continuing your relationship, always strive to be useful to her.

Once you do, it could be the difference between you never meeting that host again or you two teaming up on a great business opportunity or you individually attracting more clients than you never thought before.

9

Time To Promote & Expand Your Brand!

Your work is not done.

It's now time to get the word out about your interview.

First off, if you think the podcast host will do all of the promotion for your episode, forget it.

I've seen it from the inside through my experience working behind-the-scenes on 4 interview-based podcasts.

Typically, the most a podcast host will do is promote your episode the day it's released then it's onto the next one.

Don't worry, your interview will definitely be downloaded numerous times on the first day of release and it'll trickle downloads for the upcoming days, weeks, months and years to come as long as that podcast is alive.

However, if you want to take the promotion to another level, you'll need to take charge.

"Do your part to promote your appearance on the podcast," Buelow says. "This helps the episode stay alive and visible for longer, reaching more prospective clients. Announce that you're going to be interviewed (and that you're excited about it!). Post the finished episode on your various social media platforms, your website and your newsletter, then put the link in a rotation to keep sharing on Twitter. This also shows that you're a good guest, interested in supporting the podcast host, and they're more likely to ask you back for a future episode or recommend you to other podcasters."

Beforehand, you can ask podcast hosts how they will market your episode.

Most will say they'll promote it on social media, which is nice, but you'll want to suggest they advertise your interview to their email list too. The reason being is some podcast hosts have more engaged email subscribers than Twitter followers who would only like one of their tweets every few months.

Some ways you can promote your own episode could be via…

- Facebook Ads - https://www.Facebook.com/business/products/ads
- Instagram - https://www.Instagram.com
- LinkedIn - https://www.Linkedin.com
- Twitter - https://www.Twitter.com
- Your Own Email List

When promoting on social media, it's important to be brief, interesting and provide a link to the episode.

For example…

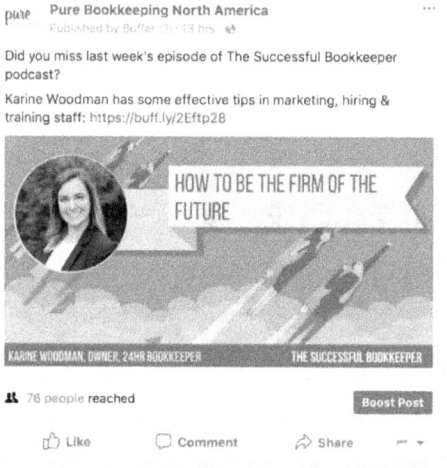

Just visit the podcast website then download the promotional image of your episode and post it alongside some written text into your social media and website.

You can also promote your episodes in your Facebook or LinkedIn group if you have one.

Of course, if you'd like to promote the old fashioned way, you can speak with your family and friends and ask them to spread the word to their relevant networks about your podcast appearance.

The lesson here is you have to make the effort to do the marketing, but it's worth it.

You now have all the tools you'll need to attract more sales leads, clients and boost your brand through your business podcast appearances.

Whether it's you putting in the time or an employee of yours, by following the previous chapters step-by-step, you can make thousands to hundreds of thousands of dollars through Podcast Guest Marketing.

You just have to follow the recipe and repeat.

In the following pages, you'll see some resources and tools that will help you get a great start.

I wish you well.

Thank you for allowing me to be a part of your journey.

Success, as always, is up to you.

10

Your Starter Podcast Contact List

So, now what?

Since you have all the tools to book your own interview-based business podcast appearances, you're ready to go, but what shows can you begin pitching to right away?

To give you a head start, here's a list of 10 various podcasts that you can contact now.

Remember, make sure whatever show you choose to connect with, it's one that is a fit for your niche.

There are no guarantees you'll appear on these podcasts, but there's nothing stopping you from giving it a shot.

Good luck!

Title: **Earn Your Happy**

Category: Health/Wellness

Contact: Francesca@loriharder.com

Website: https://www.loriharder.com

Title: **The Chalene Show**

Category: Business/Health/Self-Help

Contact: allyson@chalenejohnson.com

Website: http://www.chalenejohnson.com/podcasts/

Title: **Passive Real Estate Investing**

Category: Real Estate/Business

Contact: marco@noradarealestate.com

Website: http://www.passiverealestateinvesting.com

Title: **Fitness Professional Online**

Category: Health/Business

Contact: doug@fitnessprofessionalonline.com

Website:
https://www.fitnessprofessionalonline.com/fitness-professional-online-radio-show/

Title: **The Introvert Entrepreneur**

Category: Business/Health

Contact: beth@theintrovertentrepreneur.com

Website:
http://theintrovertentrepreneur.com/category/podcast/

Title: **Hack The Entrepreneur**

Category: Business

Contact: jon@hacktheentrepreneur.com

Website: https://hacktheentrepreneur.com

Title: **Lifetime CashFlow Through Real Estate Investing**

Category: Real Estate/Business

Contact: ron@rodkhleif.com

Website: https://rodkhleif.com/lifetime-cashflow-podcast/

Get Booked!

Title: **The Productivityist Podcast**

Category: Business

Contact: mike@productivityist.com

Website: https://productivityist.com/category/podcast/

Title: **The Productive Woman**

Category: Lifestyle/Business/Wellness

Contact: feedback@theproductivewoman.com

Website: http://www.theproductivewoman.com

Title: **Apartment Building Investing with Michael Blank**

Category: Real Estate/Business

Contact: michael@themichaelblank.com

Website: http://www.themichaelblank.com/podcasts/

Please note – Since podcasts start and shutdown all the time, the above shows and contacts are always subject to change.

11

Podcast Guest Marketing Resource Links

As you begin your podcast guest marketing journey, here are some useful links that can make your life easier.

Podcast Equipment

https://www.eofire.com/podcastequipment/

Email Marketing & Management Software

MailChimp - https://mailchimp.com

Infusionsoft - https://www.infusionsoft.com

ConvertKit - https://www.convertkit.com

AWeber - https://www.aweber.com

Article Comparing Best Email Marketing Software

https://www.businessnewsdaily.com/8276-best-email-marketing-software.html

Email List Building Tips

http://www.amyporterfield.com/category/list-building/

Podcast Interview Calling Programs

Skype - https://www.skype.com/

Zoom - https://zoom.us

Article To Help You Attract Sales Leads From Your Podcast Interview

https://www.entrepreneur.com/article/289388

Places To Find Your Business Podcasts

iTunes

https://itunes.apple.com/ca/genre/podcasts-business/id1321?mt=2

Stitcher

https://www.stitcher.com/stitcher-list/business-and-industry-podcasts-top-shows

Podbean

https://www.podbean.com/business-podcasts

PlayerFM

https://player.fm/featured/business

BlogTalkRadio

http://www.blogtalkradio.com/business

Podcast Addict App

https://play.google.com/store/apps/details?id=com.bambuna.podcastaddict&hl=en

PodcastOne

https://www.podcastone.com/technology-and-business-podcasts

NPR

https://www.npr.org/podcasts/2007/business

Listen Notes Podcast Search Engine

https://www.listennotes.com/search/?q=business&sort_by_date=0&scope=episode&offset=0&language=Any%20language&len_min=0

12

BONUS Interview Preparation Tips

The following are two quick articles I wrote to help you feel more comfortable with your business podcast interview experience.

Getting Your Voice Ready

Is this embarrassing for you?

Being unprepared for a big speech, client presentation, product launch or other important event with a lot at stake, can make you feel exposed and vulnerable.

Why do that to yourself especially when you're a guest on an interview-based business podcast that potentially has many listeners that could be your ideal customers?

Of course, research the podcast you'll be on and its audience, so you can tailor content that is useful and relevant to them.

But, here's something probably very few entrepreneurs do before their podcast appearances -- voice exercises.

If you want to effectively communicate you better warm up those pipes, so they're ready when you need them.

Here are a few exercises you can follow:

1 - Hum a song you like

2 - Vocalize some scales (Do-Re-Mi-Fa-So-La-Ti-Do)

3 - You can also loosen up your jaw by slowly saying the letters A-E-I-O-U repeatedly

4 - Tension sometimes mounts in the back of your tongue, so swish it around your mouth to relax it

The calmer your mouth is, the easier you'll be able to communicate.

The better you can speak to your ideal audience, the higher the chances they will like you and want to buy what you're offering.

So, take care of your voice and it will take care of you.

Avoid This Person

Don't be Rodney Radio.

It's a term described when a radio talk show host or DJ delivers a ridiculous voice exaggeration of how she thinks one should sound on the radio.

Don't be that person.

It just comes off as fake.

I learned this lesson back in my Radio Broadcasting college program many moons ago and it has served me well ever since.

If you're an entrepreneur who has been invited to appear as a guest on an interview-based business podcast, don't pretend to be Steve Jobs, Elon Musk or anybody else.

Be YOU.

As well, when you're in front of the microphone, don't think of the thousands of people who may potentially listen.

That might make you nervous.

Instead, just speak with one person - the podcast host.

It's a conversation, so treat it that way.

At the end of the day, when you're authentic and relaxed, you'll endear yourself to listeners, who might be future potential clients, and you'll be an enjoyable guest for the podcast host.

Acknowledgements

Podcasting has been such a gift.

Back in the summer of 2008, I'll never forget when my old basketball podcast co-host, Audley Stephenson originally pitched me the idea of creating a podcast while we sat at the Square One shopping mall food court in Mississauga, Ontario, a suburb west of Toronto.

I don't think I really heard of podcasts before then, but little did I know, agreeing to do that show would continue to have such a positive impact on me to this day.

When Audley and I performed guest booking for that podcast, I would have never guessed those skills would ever be used again, but look where I am.

Thank you Audman for helping me begin this journey.

I wouldn't have even seen the marketing value of booking entrepreneurs as guests on interview-based business podcasts if it wasn't for my mentor, client and friend, Michael Palmer.

He's the one who encouraged me to explore this world after seeing I had a skill for guest booking which would be needed by time-starved entrepreneurs who wanted to market themselves on podcasts but weren't able to do it themselves.

Thank you Michael for believing in me.

As well, I want to thank my first two Podcast Interview Experts clients, Lee Schneider and Victor Menasce for taking a chance on me.

They've been terrific to work with and there's no doubt success will always find them.

Throughout my podcasting career, I've also been blessed to learn from so many talented people including those whose insight is a part of this book including the great people who work at DigitalMarketer.com, John Lee Dumas, Amy Porterfield, Lewis Howes, Jamie Masters, Jesse Chappus and Beth Buelow.

Thank you for all the incredible content you produce.

I would also like to tip my cap to Entrepreneur.com. It gave me the chance to cover the podcasting world as a guest writer and it was a fantastic experience.

My Entrepreneur.com editor, Liz Webber was always encouraging and not afraid to let me know if an article wasn't a fit.

Thank you Liz and Entrepreneur.com for the great opportunity.

Of course, I can't forget some incredibly special people close to me.

My wife, Linda, is such an amazing and supportive woman that I am forever grateful and thankful to have her in my life.

If she wasn't around, I'd probably be working at a chicken factory.

As well, my parents and sisters are great supporters too and I'm honored to have them in my inner circle.

Finally, the person I'd like to thank the most is YOU.

I appreciate you taking the time to read this book and hopefully it gives you some actionable information that you can use right away.

You deserve to be successful.

May this resource give you the tools to get there.

About The Author

Dave is a former Entrepreneur.com podcast industry writer, current podcast host and founder of Podcast Interview Experts which is an agency that books successful entrepreneurs onto interview-based business podcasts.

During his podcasting career, he has been a guest booker for 4 shows including The Stand Out NOW! podcast which gives business owners tips on how to cut through the advertising noise to effectively reach their ideal clients.

For The Thought Leader Revolution podcast, he booked high profile guests such as Seth Godin, Barbara Corcoran and Kathy Ireland.

Back in 2008, he co-hosted The Breakdown with Dave & Audley basketball podcast where he interviewed NBA All-Stars and Basketball Hall of Fame Members.

Before his podcasting days, Dave was a former Canadian national television sports reporter where he covered the NBA, Major League Baseball and the National Hockey League.

Afterwards, he'd become a freelance entertainment writer where he'd interview the likes of Beyoncé Knowles, Jamie Foxx and Sean Astin. His work appeared in various global media outlets including ESPN.com, The Dallas Morning News and Star Wars Insider to name a few.

He would also pen his first traditionally published book using the interviews from his basketball podcast in his creation called *100 Things Raptors Fans Should Know & Do Before They Die*.

Nowadays, Dave lives in Aurora, Ontario, Canada with his lovely wife where he is still hoping the Toronto Raptors need a middle-aged 5-foot-7 sharpshooter, like himself, one day.

We invite you to join Dave on his social media networks:

LinkedIn

https://www.linkedin.com/in/davemendonca/

Twitter

https://twitter.com/DaveMendonca

Facebook

https://www.facebook.com/dave.mendonca.73

Instagram

https://www.instagram.com/davemendoncatoronto/

To receive free and valuable content about Podcast Guest Marketing and how it can help you and your business, you can join his email list by sending a message to **Dave@PodcastInterviewExperts.com**.

Are You Struggling To Find Your Ideal Clients?

Is there too much advertising noise preventing you from reaching your perfect customers?

Here's a podcast to check out…

It features marketing, publicity and sales advice, tips, suggestions, hacks, roadmaps, links and templates from top experts to help entrepreneurs connect with their future clients.

For more information visit TheStandOutNowPodcast.com.

Don't Have The Time To Book Your Own Podcast Appearances?

Visit PodcastInterviewExperts.com **or email** Dave@PodcastInterviewExperts.com **for a free consultation.**

We'll take away the hassle of getting you and your brand noticed.

www.ingramcontent.com/pod-product-compliance
Lightning Source LLC
Chambersburg PA
CBHW071321220526
45468CB00001B/457